LETTING GOD'S LOVE
GIVE YOU HOPE *in* TIMES *of* GRIEF

A *Love*
That Heals

ANGIE WINANS
GRAMMY AWARD NOMINEE

HOWARD BOOKS
A DIVISION OF SIMON & SCHUSTER
New York   London   Toronto   Sydney

Our purpose at Howard Books is to:

- Increase faith in the hearts of growing Christians
- Inspire holiness in the lives of believers
- Instill hope in the hearts of struggling people everywhere

Because He's coming again!

HOWARD
BOOKS

Published by Howard Books, a division of Simon & Schuster, Inc.
1230 Avenue of the Americas, New York, NY 10020
www.howardpublishing.com

A Love That Heals © 2008 by Angie Winans

ISBN-13: 978-1-4165-7880-2
ISBN-10:   1-4165-7880-3

10 9 8 7 6 5 4 3 2 1

Manufactured in the United States of America

For information regarding special discounts for bulk purchases,
please contact: Simon & Schuster Special Sales at 1-800-456-6798
or business@simonandschuster.com.

Edited by Between the Lines
Interior design by Tennille Paden
Photography/illustrations by Getty Images

Dedication

To those who are mourning the loss of a loved one, know that I am fully aware of your pain and heartache. It is to you that I dedicate this diary of love. I have learned a lot during my own journey, and I hope this knowledge will be a comfort to you.

I would like to begin by offering my condolences to all who have been separated from their loved ones by death. I want you to know that I realize the challenges involved in adjusting to such a loss. After experiencing the death of my brother Ronald, I felt that my love for him had betrayed me. I thought if I didn't love him so much, I wouldn't feel as much pain. Little did I know it would be because of love, specifically God's love, as God IS love, that I would be able to recover from my grief.

We know that death is inevitable. It is a part of life that we cannot avoid, and we will all face it at some point in our lives. But Love, which is God Himself, is the antidote for death. I hope that you will give God's love a chance during your journey. It is the only thing that will keep your heart safe and give you the comfort you desperately need. As you read on and journal through the following pages, I pray that you realize you are in good hands—God's hands.

Acknowledgments

To my husband, Cedric, and our children: I give my sincere thanks for your love and support. I feel so privileged to have you all in my life.

To Mom and Dad and the entire Winans family: You all mean so much to me. There's nothing like family.

To my life-long friend, Karla Mackie: You stayed close . . . right by my side, so much so that I can say, "You felt my pain," and I do realize that you loved Ronald just as much as I did. For that, I acknowledge you.

To Mimi: Thanks for being there and allowing your husband, Dirk, to be there for me also. He is truly like my brother.

To Charzet and Tina: Words cannot express our times together, and they will never be forgotten. You guys have made your mark on my heart, which can never be erased. You were there for me, in the good times and through the rough times. Thanks.

To Dr. Virgil Caldwell: You are a man whom I'm proud to call my father-in-law; a man of great wisdom, integrity and humility. I admire and respect you so very much. It is truly an honor and a delight to sit and listen and learn from you every chance I get. Thanks for such shiny and glittery intelligence; you represent Christ well.

To Bill Carpenter and JaNeen Griffin: Thanks for believing in my vision and helping me run with it. Your support will always be remembered.

To Amy J. Gregory: Thanks for taking the time to put this book into the proper format. What would I have done without you?

To my wonderful literary agent, Esther Fedorkevich: From the moment we met I knew you believed in me. Thanks for all your hard work.

Thank you Pastor Stan Mitchell for staying before God and receiving life-changing messages.

Last, but certainly not least, how could I ever say thanks to my friend, my Lord and Savior Jesus Christ? I promise I will live a life that's pleasing to you...and that is a life full of Love.

Contents

You can give without loving, but you can never love without giving.

—AMY CARMICHAEL

CHAPTER ONE

The Gift of Love

Dear Ron,

It is nearly impossible to examine the love we have in our lives without reflecting on the word *give*. The two words are closely connected from the beginning of time, when God said He so loved the world that He gave . . .

Ron, after your death God's love gave me a peace that enabled me to sleep well at night. The only reason I could stand strong was because God's love gave me strength. And the reason I can still laugh today is simply because God gave me His joy.

I believe a man's love can be measured by his giving. This truth has become more real to me as I've thought about the love you and I gave to each other. It was so rich that I must say I am content with the love we've shared here on earth.

Yes, I have been privileged to have been given so much love from all of my family. I do not take for granted what Mom and Dad gave to us. They gave us a life full of love and the blessing of happiness. And that love gives me the strength to pass on to my children and others this special gift. I want them to have what I've been given.

You know, Ron, a mutual friend of ours said some powerful words at your "homegoing celebration." He said that you had given everyone a piece of your heart until there was simply no more to give. You gave me such a wealth of love that I can live each day on the strength of those memories.

Love, Angie

A Message for You

In Joppa there was a disciple named Tabitha (which, when translated, is Dorcas), who was always doing good and helping the poor. About that time she became sick and died, and her body was washed and placed in an upstairs room. Lydda was near Joppa; so when the disciples heard that Peter was in Lydda, they sent two men to him and urged him, "Please come at once!" Peter went with them, and when he arrived he was taken upstairs to the room. All the widows stood around him, crying and showing him the robes and other clothing that Dorcas had made while she was still with them. Peter sent them all out of the room; then he got down on his knees and prayed.

—Acts 9:36–40 *NIV*

Like Dorcas, people who show their love by giving, leave a big hole in people's hearts when they die. But just as the robes and other clothing Dorcas had given freely during her life outlived her as a testament of her generous love, so your loved one's special gifts remain behind as a testament of his or her love for you. Things like . . .

- The long talks and encouraging calls when you went through that rough time
- Fixing the door that used to stick and drive you crazy
- Noticing (and loving it) when you got your hair cut
- Not eating cake when you were on your diet
- Giving you the better seat
- Choosing your favorite restaurant instead of his
- Cheering you on at your games
- Carrying your photo proudly in his wallet
- Putting her dream on hold so you could follow yours

What are some of the "gifts" your special someone left behind as a testament of his or her love for you?

_____

_____

_____

_____

_____

_____

_____

_____

_____

In what ways do these love gifts make losing someone harder?

_____

_____

_____

_____

_____

_____

In what ways do they bring comfort or soften the pain of your loss?

_____

_____

_____

_____

_____

_____

Love is an intense emotion, and when the object of that love is ripped away, it tears something deep within us. That's the reason you're hurting so much now. You've lost someone you love dearly. Perhaps worse, you've lost someone who loved you intensely—enough to care what happens to you, share your life, and give from the deepest part of the heart.

Take the time to analyze and describe how giving and receiving love from the person you lost has shaped you into being the kind of person you are today. Write your thoughts here.

_____

_____

_____

_____

_____

_____

_____

_____

_____

The gift of your loved one's life doesn't have to end with his or her death. It continues when you maintain that pattern of giving in ways that defined and truly mattered to your loved one. Imagine how he or she would feel knowing that you'll pass on what you received from him or her. How did your lost loved one give to others? Think of a cause that was dear to your loved one's heart, and support it either financially or physically. You were given a gift by having a person in your life who loved you, and you loved that person back. Use that gift to share with others.

Here's what I'll do to honor my loved one's gift of love:

_____

_____

_____

_____

_____

_____

_____

_____

But what about you, right now . . . desperately grieving the loss of one so dear? What can you do to ease the pain of the grief in your own heart when it feels as if you can hardly get out of bed and face life without that person? When Dorcas's friends were desperately grieving, they knew where to turn. They sought out Peter, a close follower and friend of Jesus. They didn't quite know how, but they believed Peter could help them.

To what friends can you turn to help you in your time of sorrow? What makes them qualified or able to walk with you on this road?

_____

_____

_____

_____

_____

Notice that Peter was really powerless in himself to do anything to help. But Peter knew the source of help and strength in times of sorrow: "He got down on his knees and prayed" (Acts 9:40 NIV). When you feel overwhelmed by sorrow, get alone with God, get on your knees, and pray. For "God is our merciful Father and the source of all comfort. He comforts us in all our troubles" (2 Corinthians 1:3–4). He's reaching out to you today with that same comfort. Won't you turn to Him today and let Him hold you in the strong arms of His love?

Reflections

A Prayer for You

Dear Lord,

Thank you for the most precious gift You gave to us, Your Son. Through this sacrifice You taught us the immeasurable worth and meaning of love. You showed us firsthand what it means to give love. Help us now, in our time of struggle, to remember the gifts our loved ones left behind that serve as examples of how much love they had for us. May we be reminded of their warmth and compassion even though our hearts may be breaking. And may we not be so overwhelmed by grief that we stop giving love to others who are with us. Teach us, in Your own special way, how to give and receive love. Amen.

The language of love is spoken

with a look, a touch, a sigh, a kiss

and sometimes a word.

—FRANK TYGER

Trust in the dark, trust in the light, trust at night and trust in the morning, and you will find that the faith which may begin perhaps by a mighty effort, will end, sooner or later, by becoming the easy and natural habit of the soul.

—HANNAH WHITALL SMITH

Trusting God

Dear Ron,

Today my thoughts go back to what you told me years ago, after your heart surgery. You said, "*I'm glad it was me on that operating table instead of one of you all, because I would not have been able to stand it.*" You said that the thought of losing one of your siblings was inconceivable. Then you asked me, "*How did it feel being one of the nine, waiting and waiting, in that waiting room?*"

"Awful," I replied. "It was one of the worst days of my life."

Now while that was true, a greater Truth was also present. I had the assurance that I was being held in God's hands—that somehow, as terrible as that day was, I could trust Him and rest in His presence.

And this is what has gotten me through losing you. Knowing that I can trust God has given me a comfort I never could have imagined, and I want you to know that had it been one of us instead of you, you *would* have been able to make it through the loss—because God would be holding you in the palm of His hand.

Love, Angie

A Message for You

Another messenger arrived with this news: "Your [Job's] sons and daughters were feasting in their oldest brother's home. Suddenly, a powerful wind swept in from the wilderness and hit the house on all sides. The house collapsed, and all your children are dead. I am the only one who escaped to tell you." Job stood up and tore his robe in grief. Then he shaved his head and fell to the ground to worship. He said, "I came naked from my mother's womb, and I will be naked when I leave. The LORD gave me what I had, and the LORD has taken it away. Praise the name of the LORD!" In all of this, Job did not sin by blaming God.

—Job 1:18–22

Did you read that? Job sounds like a saint, doesn't he? Job had suffered an incomprehensible series of tragic losses in quick succession—his wealth, his livelihood, and finally, all ten of his children in one cruel blow. I saw how deeply my parents grieved the loss of just one child when my brother Ron died—I can't fathom how any parent could keep from being totally overwhelmed by the loss of all of his or her children at the same time.

It's right to be impressed and a little awed by such a response to great loss: "The LORD gave me what I had, and the LORD has taken it away. Praise the name of the LORD!" (Job 1:21). It's also understandable if Job's response offends or even angers you. You are, after all, grieving the loss of someone so important to you that it's worth significant anger and grief. How could Job so quickly resign himself to the loss of his children? Didn't he love them and care for them as much as you love the one you lost?

Of course he did. Earlier in the chapter, we're shown how much care Job took to safeguard his children, rising early to offer a sacrifice for each one in case he or she had sinned. And notice Job's immediate response to the sad news of his children's deaths in Job 1:20. He tore his robe in grief and shaved his head, both symbols of immense grief in the culture of the Bible. Job's sorrow was real. It was deep. Still, his next response was to fall to the ground to worship God. Apparently Job's past experience and relationship with God had taught him that God was worthy of his trust and confidence—no matter what. In fact, that relationship was the only thing Job had—or that we have—that could never be taken from him. In anger and grief, Job could have rejected that relationship and God himself, but instead he chose to launch himself into God's arms.

It's the same choice you have today. Will you run to God in your grief, trusting Him to hold you, keep you, strengthen and comfort you, or will you run from Him, angry that He allowed this happen to your loved one—to you?

What is your greatest obstacle to fully trusting God, His love, His goodness, and His plan for your life in this time of loss?

_____

_____

_____

_____

_____

_____

When we lose a loved one, in addition to all the emotional upheaval of grief, we often find ourselves in an emotional tug-of-war with people around us. Some, like Job's wife, view loss as proof that God is not worthy of our trust—that He's either unable or unwilling to shield us from harm. "Are you still trying to maintain your integrity?" Job's wife pressured him. "Curse

God and die" (Job 2:9). For you it might be a friend or loved one—or even a little voice in your own head—telling you, *What good did trusting God do? Go ahead—be angry at, run from, reject a God who couldn't or wouldn't help you when you needed Him most. Serves Him right.* But that would harm only you, not God. And it makes even less sense than it would to abandon your father because you're angry and hurt that your mother died.

Has anyone pushed you to blame or reject God for not sparing your lost loved one? If so, what do you think might cause such anger or withdrawal? What role might that person's own hurt and sorrow play in such a response? How do you respond to such emotion?

_____

_____

_____

_____

_____

_____

How did Job respond to this inducement to abandon God when life got tough? He knew it was foolishness. Job told his wife, "You talk like a foolish woman. Should we accept only good things from the hand of God and never anything bad?" (Job 2:10).

We know from just looking around us that no one can

get through life unscathed. Everyone suffers disappointment, sickness, and loss. Every soldier who prayed for God to spare his life during the American Civil War is dead today. Everyone dies: it's part of life. Good *and* bad happen to every soul on earth. It's just that we want the good now and the bad . . . well, never.

When we are forced to endure those bad times, especially the unrivaled badness of losing a loved one, it's important to remember the good things God has given us and done for us through the years and to remember that God hasn't changed, even though circumstances have. He still loves you and is still worthy of your love and trust.

What are some of the good things you—and your loved one—have experienced in life? Remember that these are gifts from God.

_____

_____

_____

_____

_____

_____

Job's responses and his steadfast expressions of trust in God in the face of loss may seem unattainable to ordinary people like you and me. His stubborn refusal to question God's power and goodness or buy into the lie that Job himself was somehow to blame for his own suffering can be summed up by his emotional declaration in Job 13:15: "Though he slay me, yet will I hope in him" (NIV).

But don't fool yourself that such trust in God was always the easy response for Job. Can you identify with any of these feelings Job expressed?

- "Why is life given to those with no future, those God has surrounded with difficulties? I cannot eat for sighing; my groans pour out like water. What I always feared has happened to me. What I dreaded has come true. I have no peace, no quietness. I have no rest; only trouble comes." (Job 3:23–26)

- "I don't have the strength to endure. I have nothing to live for. Do I have the strength of a stone? Is my body made of bronze? No, I am utterly helpless, without any chance of success." (Job 6:11–13)

- "I think, 'My bed will comfort me, and sleep will ease my misery,' but then you shatter me with dreams and terrify me with visions. I would rather be strangled—rather die than suffer like this. I hate my life and don't want to go on living." (Job 7:13–16)

Far from the caricature of a tower of strength that your Sunday-school teacher may have drawn for you of Job, the true, historical man was not so different from you. He had moments of strength and great spiritual clarity, but at other times he struggled. So much so that his "friends" who came to "comfort" him actually ended up attacking him for the "unspiritual" way in which he expressed those struggles.

"I cannot keep from speaking," Job defended himself in chapter 7, verse 11. "I must express my anguish. My bitter soul must complain."

And again: "Don't I have a right to complain? Don't wild donkeys bray when they find no grass, and oxen bellow when they have no food? Don't people complain about unsalted food?" (Job 6:5–6).

In other words, it's perfectly understandable when people—or even animals—complain about small things, even those that can be remedied easily; surely God understands when we complain and express our displeasure over something so important, so devastating, as losing our precious loved one.

The good news is that God does understand. He didn't condemn Job for his struggle (see Job 42:7), and He doesn't judge us when, overwhelmed by grief, we give vent to frustration and anger. Even when Job's words were at their harshest—harsh enough to rattle his "godly" friends, who didn't want their comfortable worldview (that if you do good, God will do good to you and keep you from suffering) shattered—Job never lost faith and confidence in God. Even as he longed for God to kill him and relieve him of his unrelenting suffering, Job took comfort from his faithfulness to and trust in God. "At least I can take comfort in this: Despite the pain, I have not denied the words of the Holy One" (Job 6:10). In the New International Version, Job describes this continuing trust in God as his "joy in unrelenting pain."

When we experience the loss of a loved one, God may seem absent, because death is so very real, and its reality may overpower our feeling the presence of God. As a result, sometimes the last thing we want to do is turn to God. But we shouldn't let grief distance us from our heavenly Father. It should lead us toward the only real place we can go in such trying times—to Him.

Write a prayer to God, asking Him to help you remain faithful and trusting in Him as you go through the grieving process.

_____

_____

_____

_____

_____

_____

Be aware that grieving isn't an orderly, linear journey through the seven stages of grief: (1) shock or disbelief, (2) denial, (3) bargaining, (4) guilt, (5) anger, (6) depression, and (7) acceptance/hope. Instead, it's two steps forward, one step back. We may swing from anger to guilt to hope and back to denial. You may skip a stage, race through some stages but get stuck in another or feel like you're experiencing all the emotions at once. You may get discouraged to find yourself returning to a stage you thought you'd finished. It's okay . . . you're normal. Even if it seems you're regressing, you're probably not.

Sometimes people are so shocked at losing a loved one that they respond initially with great strength and unshakeable faith in God. But then, as time goes on and the reality of living with the loss sets in, the emotional wearing that comes from grief can unexpectedly catapult them into anger or denial. It's important to recognize that as we grieve, we'll go through the stages of grief in our own time and in our own way. We mustn't feel guilty if we don't progress according to someone else's timetable or respond in the same way as someone else—even someone who loved and lost the same person we did.

What stages of the grieving process have you been through? Where are you now? What's the most difficult part about grieving? The most unsettling part?

_____

_____

_____

_____

_____

_____

_____

_____

_____

_____

_____

Wherever you are in your grieving process, the most important thing is not to stop trusting in God's power and goodness. Go ahead and shout! Tell Him how unfair it feels, ask Him why He let this happen. He understands. But never close your heart to Him.

Trusting God in our grief can be difficult because we might think it was He who took our loved one away from us. He's God, after all. Even if He didn't "smite" your loved one, surely He could have kept this from happening.

But even now God is worthy of your trust. He is good. He is powerful. He is concerned about you and feels the pain of your loss. No matter how you rail against Him, He won't abandon you. He is there for you. He loves you. He is working on your behalf, comforting, healing, and bringing good even out of this dark situation.

Take comfort in the words of the psalmist, perhaps learned in the fires of suffering and loss: "God is our refuge and strength, an ever-present help in trouble. Therefore we will not fear, though the earth give way and the mountains fall into the heart of the sea, though its waters roar and foam and the mountains quake with their surging" (Psalm 46:1–3 NIV).

Grief is painful, but God is present. Grief feels overwhelming, but God is right beside you, even when you can't feel Him. Grief brings a river of tears, but God is close, sheltering you with His hands. You can trust your grieving heart to Him because He is faithful. He will never leave or forsake you (see Hebrews 13:5).

Left to our own resources, our strength will falter. But when we trust in God, we will be able to survive and come through grief whole.

What evidence have you seen of God's loving presence in the midst of grief? How have you felt His hand overshadowing your life?

_____

_____

_____

_____

_____

_____

A Prayer for You

Dear Lord,

Thank You for giving us the opportunity to trust in You. Thank You that we have sufficient reason to trust in You and Your divine goodness. Help us in our weakness to rest in Your presence more fully as each day passes. May we not forget that Your mercies are new every morning and that Your faithfulness reaches beyond the skies. May we allow You to take our pains, hurts, and aches and put them into Your hands with confidence that they are in the best place they can be. And thank You that You understand what we're going through. May we be reminded of the suffering of Your only Son, and may it open our eyes to the reality that You understand all things, even the terrible pain of loss. Amen.

The feeling remains that

God is on the journey too.

—*Teresa of Ávila*

*E*arth has no sorrow that

heaven cannot heal.

—*THOMAS MOORE*

CHAPTER THREE

The Promise of Joy

Dear Ron,

After your funeral in Detroit, Michigan, I couldn't imagine catching my
back home to Nashville, Tennessee. I didn't know how I would continu
the way it was before your death. I couldn't understand how I would be
to continue being a good wife and mother to my husband and children.
unsure what type of daughter I would turn out to be for my parents.
certain I didn't have the strength to be a good friend to my friends.

You see, Ronald, after I lost you, grief tried to destroy me. Sorrow atten
to overcome my soul. But God made sure my sadness did not consume m
formed a circle of protection around my fragile heart.

It is because of Him that I was able to resume being the wife and mon
I once was to my husband and children. It is because of Him that I can be
for our parents. It's because of Him that I can be a good friend to others.
has taken what I was certain would crush me and somehow wielded His
and comfort in such a way as to restore joy in my life. I can smile. I can la
can rejoice. Yes, I still miss you, Ron. But God has turned my sorrow into

As a result of all I've been through since your death, I've developed a z
share with others the peace that I've experienced in my time of need. To co
all those who mourn, to help bind up the brokenhearted. To let them know
God will give beauty for their ashes, the oil of joy for their sorrow.

So, for the sake of those whose hearts are broken, I will not rest. And
those who mourn, I will not be silent until the message of God's goodnes
forth in brightness and the love of God, as a lamp that burns. God is a
God . . . even in the midst of pain.

Love, Angie

A Message for You

Martha said to Jesus, "Lord, if only you had been here, my brother would not have died. But even now I know that God will give you whatever you ask." Jesus told her, "Your brother will rise again." "Yes," Martha said, "he will rise when everyone else rises, at the last day." Jesus told her, "I am the resurrection and the life. Anyone who believes in me will live, even after dying. Everyone who lives in me and believes in me will never ever die."

—*John 11:21–26*

Where was Jesus when you really needed Him? While Lazarus had lived, his sisters, Martha and Mary, still had hope. They sent word to Jesus: "Lord, the one you love is sick" (John 11:3 NIV). Surely Jesus would rush to His friend's bedside and heal him. But four long, agonizing days went by before Jesus arrived, and by then it was too late. Lazarus was dead. Read the whole story for yourself in John 11:1–44. It'll give you hope and comfort, but first it might make you mad.

When Jesus got to Bethany and joined the crowd at Lazarus's funeral, the question of the day was really a subtle accusation: "This man healed a blind man. Couldn't he have kept Lazarus from dying?" (John 11:37).

Martha and Mary both had the same thought but said it more nicely: "Lord, if only you had been here, my brother would not have died" (Martha in John 11:21, Mary in 11:32).

Have you ever leveled that accusation at Jesus? "Lord, surely You could have kept my loved one from dying. Why weren't You here when I needed You?" Express your feelings on this subject to God here.

_____

_____

_____

_____

_____

Did Martha know that when Jesus received her urgent message, He stayed where He was for two more days before coming to her? Maybe, maybe not. Perhaps she knew it wouldn't have mattered much. Given that Lazarus had been dead four days when Jesus arrived, it's likely Lazarus died shortly after the message was sent. A two-day delay surely wouldn't have made any difference. Still . . . this was important . . . a matter of life and death. If Jesus loved Lazarus, why would He delay at all? It's enough to make one feel unimportant, abandoned, hurt.

In spite of her obvious sorrow and her disappointment that Jesus hadn't been there when she most needed Him, Martha made a bold declaration of faith and trust in Jesus that must have delighted Him: "But even now I know that God will give you whatever you ask" (John 11:22).

Have you ever felt disappointed or betrayed by God's apparent lack of presence or effort on your behalf when your loved one was dying? Have you forgiven Him yet? If so, express that here, along with any declaration of faith in God's faithfulness and ability to help and deliver. How does it feel to verbalize that?

_____

_____

_____

_____

_____

_____

_____

_____

Instead of keeping her brother from dying, Jesus spoke words of encouragement, comfort, and hope to Martha. "I am the resurrection and the life. Anyone who believes in me will live, even after dying. Everyone who lives in me and believes in me will never ever die. Do you believe this, Martha?" (John 11:25–26).

Do *you* believe this? Is it harder or easier to believe after losing your loved one? Journal your thoughts.

_____

_____

_____

_____

_____

_____

_____

Martha believed. "I have always believed you are the Messiah, the Son of God" (John 11:27). And her faith—like yours—would not be disappointed.

The highlight of this story is that Jesus raised Lazarus from the dead in a dramatic moment in front of a whole crowd. Imagine how exciting it must have been to witness that! Imagine the sheer joy that must have swept over the crowd, chasing grief and sorrow completely away. The knowledge that Jesus can raise the dead is the part of the story that gives us comfort and hope. The part of the story that could make me angry (at least a little resentful) is that someone got to hug her brother again, but not me. What I wouldn't give to have Ronald back.

You probably understand that feeling. You may have felt that way yourself; maybe when someone with the same condition as your loved one made it, while your loved one didn't. Anger in the face of death is natural. Jesus Himself felt anger at Lazarus's death (see John 11:33, 38) even though He knew that in a matter of minutes He was going to raise Lazarus from the dead. Death should make us angry. It's an outrage against the way God intended things to be (Romans 5:12 tells us that sin entered the world through one man, Adam, and death through sin).

Knowing His loved one would live again didn't keep Jesus from being angry. It didn't keep Him from weeping in bitter sorrow either (see John 11:35). But as believers, we don't have to grieve like people who have no hope (see 1 Thessalonians 4:13).

For believers, death is only a prelude to life. Don't feel guilty about your anger or sorrow at the death of your loved one. But don't be afraid to rejoice either. Death is but a doorway—a doorway to eternal, glorious, joyful life. And that's worth celebrating.

It's worth celebrating that Jesus has power over death. He has defeated it. Whether a person is dead four days, like Lazarus, or longer, like your loved one, death cannot keep in the grave anyone who believes and lives in Jesus. The outcome is assured—it's only a matter of time. "Our dying bodies must be transformed into bodies that will never die; our mortal bodies must be transformed into immortal bodies. Then, when our dying bodies have been transformed into bodies that will never die, this Scripture will be fulfilled: 'Death is swallowed up in victory. O death, where is your victory? O death, where is your sting?'" (1 Corinthians 15:53–55).

In the middle of trouble, sadness, despair, hopelessness . . . in the midst of darkness, when all seems lost . . . when the sun has lost its radiance . . . when your heart is troubled, you *can* have joy and gladness. Your heart will not grieve forever. You are not at the end of the story. In the end there is victory and life. "Weeping may last through the night, but joy comes with the morning" (Psalm 30:5).

How does that verse make you feel?

_____

_____

_____

_____

_____

How close to the morning of joy would you say you are right now? Describe your journey.

_____

_____

_____

_____

_____

_____

Have you experienced God's assurance of His victory over death—a time when your heart was flooded with joy and peace even more than by the painful sting of losing your loved one? Describe that experience.

_____

_____

_____

_____

_____

_____

_____

_____

The pain and heartache that come along with losing a loved one can be intense, even unbearable. At times it can seem impossible to imagine ever healing from the tragedy or being truly happy again. It can even seem that God isn't present, because the pain feels unendurable. Some people don't turn to God for comfort, because they don't believe He can transform their sadness into joy. It seems impossible. But it's not.

My heart was shattered into a million tiny pieces when my brother died. I struggled to find enough emotional equilibrium to make it through even one day. I knew that something had to change drastically for me, or I'd ruin my health. Something had to anchor my spirit so my heart could function at the pace my life demanded. I needed not only to put my trust in God but also to trust Him that the pain of losing Ron would decrease. That my tears would not well up and spill down my cheeks every five minutes. That I could begin to live again without lugging around the weight of grief on my back.

I am a living and breathing witness that sorrow can be transformed into joy. God Himself makes this possible. He wants His children's lives to be full of joy. The joy I speak of is deeper than happiness. Happiness depends on our circumstances, but joy is something you can have even now, in the face of that old enemy, death.

Have you experienced times when things weren't going your way, but because you leaned on God, the joy in your heart exceeded the sorrow of your hardship? Write about it here.

_____

_____

_____

_____

_____

_____

In spite of the loss of your loved one, what are some things that still bring you joy?

_____

_____

_____

_____

_____

_____

Though weeping has its season, joy is sure to follow. God is a God of goodness. He does not leave our hearts broken forever. He does not allow our tears to flow without end. The things that cause us pain do not last forever. No, "God blesses those who mourn, for they will be comforted" (Matthew 5:4).

A Prayer for You

Dear Lord,

Teach us how to dance even when our chests throb with pain from broken hearts. Keep us steady when our world has been abruptly shaken by a tsunami of sorrow. Take our hands when storms leave us cold and trembling. Weave Your comfort into our mourning. Remind us that even grief is temporary but Your Word and Your love are unfailing and eternal. Show us how to trust in You so we can become living testimonies that we will not be consumed by sadness but that joy does come in the morning. Teach us how to breathe and live in the moment so that Your goodness can have its way in our lives and transform even the saddest of situations into something that is good. Amen.

The deeper that sorrow carves into your being, the more joy you can contain. Is not the cup that holds your wine the very cup that was burned in the potter's oven?

—*Kahlil Gibran*

It is up to us to live up to the legacy

that was left for us, and to leave a legacy

that is worthy of our children

and of future generations.

—CHRISTINE GREGOIRE

A Living Legacy

Dear Ron,

You certainly had quite a way about you. You could lighten even the grimmest of situations and moods with a joke or a reminder not to take things too seriously. And you lived your life well. You were benevolent and sacrificial. Your attitude was positive regardless of circumstances. You had a tenderness that was soothing to those who needed to be comforted. You had a passionate spirit that could melt the calloused hearts of cynics. You had a faith that could wrestle with and not be shaken by the toughest questions. With these things, you touched the lives of many people, me included.

Not only was I personally impacted and made better by the way you lived your life and shared your gifts with me, but you inspired me to follow your example. I can't copy who you are, Ron, that's for sure; but I can take what I learned from your life and use it in a way that carries on your legacy. I try to be more patient now because of you. I laugh more and have more fun with my kids and my husband because of you. I take my life's calling more seriously because of you. I love more. I give more. I trust more. I rejoice more. I forgive more. I do these things because you taught me how. And through me, your spirit lives on. The legacy of your life has been passed down to me.

For this I am grateful beyond words. You used your time on earth wisely and chose to live a life worthy of the calling of God. It makes me so proud of who you are, and motivates me to better myself every day. What a life! What a legacy!

Love, Angie

A Message for You

*Keep putting into practice all you learned and received from me—
everything you heard from me and saw me doing.*

—Philippians 4:9

Did you know that if you write about your problems to "Dear Abby," you're actually writing to "Abby's" daughter, Jeanne Phillips? Pauline Esther Friedman Phillips, the original "Abby," was forced to retire in 2002 as she battled Alzheimer's disease. Jeanne picked up right where her mother left off, dispensing commonsense wisdom to people needing help. That's some family legacy.

Did you also know that from 1943 until the late 1990s, the legacy of playing the collie "Lassie" on television and film was carried on by eight generations of dogs descended from the original canine hero named Pal in real life? The dogs had to look enough like their father that no one would notice the switch. They also had to be bigger than typical collies so the child stars who played opposite them wouldn't outgrow them too quickly. I guess you could call that the "Lassie Legacy."

When Kansas City's "Secret Santa," Larry Stewart, revealed his identity—and that he was dying of cancer—after twenty-six years of handing out significant sums of cash to strangers in need, several people felt inspired to carry on his legacy. Any Christmas, if you visit Kansas City, you just might see one of these generous people handing out multiple hundred-dollar bills. Larry Stewart's legacy of love and generosity has outlived him.

It has been said that God never allows a great man or woman to die without passing the torch to someone else. That's called a legacy. It's what Moses passed on to Joshua:

> After the death of Moses the servant of the LORD, the LORD said to Joshua son of Nun, Moses' aide: "Moses my servant is dead. Now then, you and all these people, get ready to cross the Jordan River into the land I am about to give them—to the Israelites. I will give you every place where you set your foot, as I promised Moses. . . . No one will be able to stand up against you all the days of your life. As I was with Moses, so I will be with you; I will never leave you nor forsake you. Be strong and courageous, because you will lead these people to inherit the land I swore to their forefathers to give them." (Joshua 1:1–3, 5–6 NIV)

Moses was one of the greatest men of the Bible. God used him to free the Israelites from slavery in Egypt. He was the channel through whom God gave the laws upon which Western civilization has been built. He led a ragtag band of approximately two million people on a journey that lasted more than forty years. But just as God was ready to lead the people into the Promised Land of Canaan, Moses died.

Your loved one was a great person too. He or she might not have had the résumé Moses did, but who your loved one was and what he or she did was important. What are some of the things your loved one did that made him or her great?

_____

_____

_____

_____

_____

_____

What more might your loved one have done or accomplished had his or her life not been shortened by death?

_____

_____

_____

_____

_____

_____

What might God be calling you to do to take up the mantle, finish the work, or carry on the legacy of your loved one? Are you willing to do so?

_____

_____

_____

_____

_____

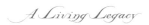

If you're willing, God is able. You don't have to be afraid that you're not good enough to continue the tasks to which God has called you. It's God's work, even if it's secular or mundane. He will be with you, helping you. Insert the name of your loved one and embrace this as God's promise to you: "As I was with _____, so I will be with you; I will never leave you nor forsake you" (Joshua 1:5 NIV).

Read Joshua 1:1–9 in the Bible. How many times did God tell Joshua to be strong and courageous? Why should that reassure you as you contemplate picking up where your loved one left off?

_____

_____

_____

_____

_____

_____

_____

Maybe this legacy is something you'll have to grow into. Your loved one was at this awhile. You don't have to measure up to who he or she was or what he or she did—just do your best. Be you. Put your own spin on things. Maybe your loved one wrote encouraging notes, but you're not a writer. That's okay. Give people a cheery call instead.

Or perhaps your loved one served meals at a homeless shelter, but that's not you. Maybe you can give haircuts or donate food, clothes, or supplies to help people at the same shelter. You're still living out the legacy of helping the needy that you saw modeled by your loved one.

Joshua wasn't the leader Moses was, but he was great at being Joshua. Both men were great leaders who played to their individual strengths to accomplish the jobs God had called them to do. Joshua was undoubtedly strengthened and enabled by the forty years he spent as Moses' closest aide. He watched a great leader in action. He learned how Moses did things. He saw the importance of maintaining a close relationship with God and obeying Him. In fact, in Joshua 1:7–8, God reminded Joshua of these keys to success. The same strategy will work for you as you live out your loved one's good legacy. From this passage, summarize the keys to success.

_____

_____

_____

_____

_____

_____

_____

_____

How regularly do you read, meditate on, and act upon God's Word? How important is this as you live out the legacy of your loved one?

_____

_____

_____

_____

_____

_____

Our loved ones left behind more than memories or snapshots in their lives, images of moments they shared with us. They left heirlooms of who they were, what they did, how they lived, what they believed in, and what mattered most to them. They left us with the memories of what they wanted their lives to stand for.

What does carrying on our loved ones' legacies mean? It's more than just remembering them. It's living out the life lessons we learned from them, sharing with others the gifts they offered, and making a difference with our own lives.

Take the time to think about the life of your loved one. What was the focus of his or her life? What did his or her life mean to you?

_____

_____

_____

_____

_____

_____

_____

I often share with people how Ron was a great example of what our lives can become when we use our God-given talents and abilities to serve Him. Ron was an amazing singer, songwriter, and performer. We shared many a stage together, and Ron was the one who helped me to hone my own musical gifts. He taught me many things in this arena, not just how to perform well but also how to honor God through the gifts He has given me. Though Ron was extremely talented, he was not egotistical about his abilities. He used them to minister to people. He used them to encourage people who were struggling or enduring hardship. He used them to demonstrate how God could work in the lives of those who gave such gifts back to God as an offering.

This is a message that has been ingrained in the Winans family through Ron's wisdom. It prevents us from glorifying ourselves and moves us to thank God for giving us the abilities we have. It is also a message that I continually share with my own children and others in the music business. And it's a message that forms the basis of how I use my gifts. This is how I carry on a part of Ron's legacy.

What is one of the most important life values your loved one taught you? How, and in what ways, do (or will) you put it into

practice? How does actively living your loved one's legacy help you to move through the healing process?

_____

_____

_____

_____

_____

Even now that your loved one is gone, it's easy to remember how he or she inspired you to be a better person and live a better life. You see a news story that you know would have been of special interest. You know what he would have done to help when a tree falls on your neighbor's house. You can imagine the comfort she would have given when a friend tells you she's getting divorced.

Your loved one is gone; you can't change that. But you can be just as helpful, just as kind, as loving, as constant, as comforting. You can be a living legacy that will honor the life of your loved one every day.

Read Philippians 4:8–9 as if it were a message from your loved one just to you: "Dear brothers and sisters, one final thing. Fix your thoughts on what is true, and honorable, and right, and pure, and lovely, and admirable. Think about things that are excellent and worthy of praise. Keep putting into practice all you learned and received from me—everything you heard from me and saw me doing. Then the God of peace will be with you."

What is the legacy you want to leave behind for your loved ones? A legacy of faith? A legacy of love? A legacy of hope? A legacy of healing? All of the above?

Meditate on your own life. Be inspired by the legacy your loved one left for you, and write your own legacy. There are many ways you can do this. Experts suggest writing what they call a "legacy letter." This is a love letter to the future that you can leave behind for your loved ones. It describes who you are, what your beliefs are, what you value most, what life lessons you've learned, and how you want to be remembered. Here are some questions and things to consider that you can include in this testament of your life:

- Express appreciation of and to those people who shaped your life for the better or brought into your life special joys, memories, and happiness.
- What matters most to you about your life? your spirituality? your family? your vocation? helping others? volunteering?
- Share the life lessons you learned from both good and bad experiences.
- Express regrets, apologies, or forgiveness to people you may have hurt or with whom you experienced misunderstandings.
- Grieve past losses, and write about what you're looking forward to accomplishing and seeing come to fruition in the future.

- Share the story of your relationship with God. How did you find Him? How did He seek you out? What does your spirituality mean to you?
- Write the story of your life—who you were, who you have become. How do you want others to understand you and the life you live?
- Write about the legacies left by loved ones who have already died. What have you learned from their experience? How do you carry on what you have learned from them?

Express some of these things in the space below.

_____

_____

_____

_____

_____

_____

_____

_____

_____

_____

_____

_____

_____

A Prayer for You

Dear Lord,

As our tears still need to be wiped dry, as our hearts still ache from the loss, and as our memories keep alive the spirit of our loved ones, may we remember the value of their lives. Help us to better treasure their gifts that inspired improvement in ourselves. Jesus, just as You lived a life full of promise and meaning and instructed us to follow in Your footsteps, so may we do the same in honor of the ones we've lost. And Lord, may this serve as a reminder to live godly and purposeful lives. May we not forget that what we do and the way we live do matter. May we live in such a way that the legacies we leave behind are ones that will not be forgotten but will inspire others to live them out in their own special ways. Amen.

Our days are numbered.
One of the primary goals
in our lives should be to prepare for our last
day. The legacy we leave is not just in our
possessions, but in the quality of our lives.
What preparations should we be
making now? The greatest waste in
all of our earth, which cannot be recycled
or reclaimed, is our waste of the time
that God has given us each day.

—BILLY GRAHAM

Pleasure is the flower that passes;

remembrance, the lasting perfume.

—JEAN DE BOUFFLERS

Healing Memories

Dear Ron,

So many warm memories flood my mind from time to time. You know, you were the one who taught me to cherish special moments in my life. You always had an amazing way of remembering not just momentous occasions but ordinary moments too—drinking endless cups of coffee with me and laughing, playing games with my children, singing songs around the piano with our siblings for no special reason. You gave me the precious gift of remembering, and it has served me well, especially since you went away.

Sometimes when the pain of losing you begins to overwhelm me, I think about the great times we had. At first this was difficult because it seemed as if remembering only magnified the pain. But as time went on, the tears over the memories you stamped on my heart turned into smiles, joy, even laughter.

One special memory is how you convinced me to learn sign language so we could be a part of our church's deaf ministry. I thought you were crazy, but, boy, how getting involved in that changed my life! And I have you to thank. Some of the best times happened in that small classroom where we learned how to sign. Your enthusiasm and patience definitely helped me in the learning process. I remember how much signing meant to you. And I was reminded of how much it meant to me, too, when you were lying on your deathbed and signed "I love you" just moments before you passed on.

I always think about you, Ron. I always remember the good times we had. And though it makes me miss you, it makes me feel good knowing we shared so much in this life and that I have so much to remember you by.

Love, Angie

A Message for You

The people left their camp to cross the Jordan, and the priests who were carrying the Ark of the Covenant went ahead of them. It was the harvest season, and the Jordan was overflowing its banks.

—Joshua 3:14–15

Has a season of harsh reaping come to your life? When every growing thing that once produced fruit has been cut away, and rivers of sorrow and difficulty are overflowing the banks, threatening to overwhelm your heart with grief? The people of Israel were in a similar spot when they approached the torrential, angry Jordan River at flood stage. Like you, they stood at a crossroads: the nexus of two very different realities. Behind them lay the long, hard desert of the past. Their journey had included exhilarating mountaintop victories and painful valleys of disappointment and defeat. Through it all, Moses—their leader, their example, and their spiritual father—had walked beside them. But now he was gone, buried on a mountaintop with only a view of the longed-for Promised Land. The next steps they took would be on their own.

Before them lay an uncertain future. God's Promised Land was blocked by a seemingly insurmountable obstacle: they would have to cross the river at the worst possible time. You may understand the feeling—standing in an uncomfortable limbo between the past and the future, unable to go back, incapable of moving forward . . . uncertain . . . fearful . . . weary . . . numb.

But no river is a match for our God, not even the river of death that separates us from those we love. When we stand on the banks of that Great River for ourselves or to say good-bye to a loved one, we can remember what Joshua told the people of Israel as they stood at the edge of the Jordan: "Today you will know that the living God is among you" (Joshua 3:10).

What evidence have you seen of God's presence even in the midst of your difficult loss?

_____

_____

_____

_____

_____

_____

When the priests carried the Ark of the Covenant, the symbol of God's presence among His people, into the swollen, raging waters of the Jordan, the waters stopped. The people were not swallowed up, washed away, or drowned. Miraculously, they were able to cross a seemingly impassible river, not just safely but on dry ground (see Joshua 3:15–17).

Then God gave Joshua unusual instructions:

> When all the people had crossed the Jordan, the Lord said to Joshua, "Now choose twelve men, one from each tribe. Tell them, 'Take twelve stones from the very place where the priests are standing in the middle of the Jordan. Carry them out and pile them up at the place where you will camp tonight.'"
>
> So Joshua called together the twelve men he had

chosen. . . . He told them, "Go into the middle of the Jordan, in front of the Ark of the Lord your God. Each of you must pick up one stone and carry it out on your shoulder—twelve stones in all, one for each of the twelve tribes of Israel. We will use these stones to build a memorial. In the future your children will ask you, 'What do these stones mean?' Then you can tell them, 'They remind us that the Jordan River stopped flowing when the Ark of the Lord's Covenant went across.' These stones will stand as a memorial among the people of Israel forever." (Joshua 4:1–7)

The stones, smooth from the rushing waters of the Jordan, were a monument and a memorial to a significant event and a powerful presence—God's! This memorial would stand as a permanent testament acknowledging both the bad and the good: the difficult circumstances, the emotional journey through, and God's power and faithfulness throughout.

God understands that it's important to remember. When we lose someone special to us, not all our memories will be pleasant. Some will make us laugh; others will make us cry. But they all serve a purpose in the healing process—like individual stones in a monument to that person's life. Such memories have many roles: they warm us, encourage and inspire us, warn and challenge us, and provide example and instruction. They keep our loved ones alive in our hearts and their influence extending into the future.

Memories are like snapshots in a photo album or like individual stones snatched from the bottom of even the most turbulent river—precious stones that remind us of our journey with the loved one we lost, the terror of the river, and the assurance that God walks beside us.

What are twelve memory stones you carry with you from your journey with your loved one?

MEMORY STONE 1:

What was it about your loved one that made you love (and really like) him or her so much?

_____

_____

_____

_____

_____

MEMORY STONE 2:

Write about one memory that makes you laugh until you cry.

_____

_____

_____

_____

_____

MEMORY STONE 3:

Write about one memory that comforts you.

_____

_____

_____

_____

_____

_____

MEMORY STONE 4:

Write about a memory that helps you realize the extent of his or her love for you.

_____

_____

_____

_____

_____

_____

MEMORY STONE 5:

Write about a memory that makes you appreciate who your loved one was.

_____

_____

_____

_____

_____

_____

_____

MEMORY STONE 6:

Reminisce about a time when he or she inspired you to do
something great or life changing.

_____

_____

_____

_____

_____

_____

_____

MEMORY STONE 7:

What kind of difference did your loved one make in your life?
How did he or she do that?

_____

_____

_____

_____

_____

_____

MEMORY STONE 8:

What would you like everyone to know about your loved one?

_____

_____

_____

_____

_____

_____

MEMORY STONE 9:

What's your earliest memory of that person?

_____

_____

_____

_____

_____

_____

MEMORY STONE 10:

What's your favorite memory?

_____

_____

_____

_____

_____

_____

MEMORY STONE 11:

What memory is most symbolic of the kind of person your loved one was and the kind of relationship you had together?

_____

_____

_____

_____

_____

_____

MEMORY STONE 12:

If he or she were here right now, what memories would you likely talk about together?

_____

_____

_____

_____

_____

_____

Sometimes our monuments to our lost loved ones are mostly symbolic: a collection of memories that honor them and keep them alive in our hearts. But some memorials are more tangible. You could:

- Make a shadow box, collage, or scrapbook featuring mementos from special times together—newspaper clippings, pressed flowers from a special event, a program from a concert or play enjoyed together, birthday cards, medals earned, a birth certificate, a driver's license, a pair of glasses, a favorite ornament, etc.
- Sew a quilt made of pieces of fabric from the clothing worn by your loved one at significant times in his or her life.
- Plant a tree with special meaning or a rose bush in that person's favorite color.
- Take a class that she encouraged you to take or in a subject he wanted to master.
- Raise money to finance a scholarship, a memorial "star" or "stone," or a seat in your loved one's name at a church or organization that was near to his or her heart.

Think of your own appropriate ways to memorialize your loved one's life. Describe one or two here.

_____

_____

_____

_____

_____

_____

_____

Your loved one is gone but will never be forgotten. Even beyond you, that person's life will continue to impact others through you. As Joshua said to his people: "In the future your children will ask, 'What do these stones mean?' Then you can tell them" (Joshua 4:21–22).

You can tell people too. For what others—your children, grandchildren, his or her children—do you want to keep alive the memory of your loved one? How will you do that, and what will you tell them?

_____

_____

_____

_____

_____

_____

_____

A Prayer for You

Dear Lord,

Thank You for allowing us the incredible opportunity to have gifts from You, gifts in the form of loved ones who bring joy into our lives. What a privilege to be given such priceless presents, eternal "stones." I pray that You will help us to keep alive the memories of those we have lost. Fill our spirits and our minds with the ways they have made our lives better and with the ways they've made us become better people. May we not forget the joy they have brought into our lives. Keep them alive in our hearts, Father. Amen.

Memory is a child walking along a seashore. You never can tell what small pebble it will pick up and store away among its treasured things.

*—*PIERCE HARRIS

We are all born for love. It is the

principle of existence, and its only end.

—BENJAMIN DISRAELI

CHAPTER SIX

To Love Again

Dear Ron,

Remember how free spirited and full of love we were together? You and I were always finding new friends from all over the world to love. And we wanted our newfound friends to fall in love with us. We even made a kind of sport out of this. Our aim was to make it very hard for people to say good-bye to us. Seeing a tear in someone's eye as the person set off on a journey, leaving us behind, signaled that we had succeeded.

Our hearts were blessed to see people touched by the love we freely gave. And we were touched by their love in return. Ron, this is who we were and who I am still. Loving is a way of life to me, and I owe that to you. You taught me how to share my love with others. You also showed me how to open up and accept love from others.

After your death I was afraid to love so freely. For a long time I was cautious—I felt a need to protect myself from the heartache that sometimes comes with loving. Before I knew it, my heart closed up, and for a long time I was unable to give or receive love.

I eventually realized, though, that it's impossible to live that way. I could never survive in this world without breathing the fullness of joy and wonder that love brings. So I decided to love again. I chose to open my heart once more. And I realized again that you were right, Ronald—life is just not worth living unless you're free to love.

Love, Angie

A Message for You

Simeon blessed them, and he said to Mary, the baby's mother, "This child [Jesus] is destined to cause many in Israel to fall, but he will be a joy to many others. He has been sent as a sign from God, but many will oppose him. As a result, the deepest thoughts of many hearts will be revealed. And a sword will pierce your very soul."

—Luke 2:34–35

That last part of Simeon's prediction to Mary describes quite accurately how it feels when someone we love dearly is ripped from us by death: like a sword has pierced our very souls. Does it still feel that way to you?

Realistically, we all know that death will eventually separate us from our loved ones. Even the strongest marriage, family bonds, or friendships are subject to the chill winds of death. Unless everyone you love were to be killed at once in some freak accident, violent storm, or act of war, somebody eventually will be left behind to suffer the grief of loss.

If you knew how it would end with you and your loved one, would you have changed anything? Write your thoughts here.

_____

_____

_____

_____

_____

_____

Would you still have chosen to love that person, even knowing the pain you'd endure in losing him or her, or would you have guarded your heart and not allowed yourself to love? Why?

_____

_____

_____

_____

_____

_____

Mary was told right from the start, when her newborn Son was just days old, that loving Him would bring her sorrow and pain. But that didn't keep her from embracing Him, committing herself to be there through it all, and opening her heart fully to love Him.

When was the first time you truly understood that you would lose your loved one? How did it change the way you felt toward, treated, or responded to him or her?

_____

_____

_____

_____

_____

_____

When our hearts finally are forced to grapple with the loss of our loved ones—and our own mortality—it changes us profoundly. Some people deny it and try to pretend it isn't really happening. You might see this when people refuse to let the dying loved one talk about death or his or her own fears, or when they insist on talking about events in the distant future as if the dying loved one will still be around.

Other people become overly attentive and protective of the loved one, as if their own diligence, strength, and sheer willpower might somehow stave off the inevitable.

Knowing that we have just a short time left with a loved one creates a nagging feeling of sadness and anxiety that stretches out the grieving process almost beyond what it seems we can endure. It can make us fearful and negative. Might this infection be the one that pushes her over the edge? Will this doctor's visit bring more bad news? Could this hospital stay be the last? Will his heart give out suddenly in the night? Will I see her in the morning?

How might Mary's understanding of the loss she would face with Jesus have heightened her emotions in the following situations throughout His life?

- While on a trip, Mary and Joseph "lost" Jesus for three days, only finding Him in the temple after a frantic search (see Luke 2:41–50).

- Mary and her family couldn't get close to Jesus because of the great crowds surrounding Him (Luke 8:19).

_____

_____

_____

_____

_____

_____

_____

- Mary watched her son die from her vantage point at the foot of the cross (see John 19:25).

_____

_____

_____

_____

_____

_____

_____

Like you, Mary chose not to take the easy route—the path that would have shielded her from the full emotional trauma of Jesus' suffering and death struggle. Instead, Mary stuck with Him right to the bitter, bloody end. She witnessed the jeers and taunts of the angry crowds; she was pierced by the abuse that had made His beloved features almost unrecognizable; she was crushed by the knowledge that she'd never again hold her little boy in her arms or feel the warmth of His breath when He kissed her cheek.

Mary could have left and spared herself that pain, but she didn't. Why? Because she loved Him. She loved Him too much to let Him go through it without her.

Maybe you walked with your loved one for a long time through the valley of the shadow of death. Or perhaps you were blindsided by a sudden, unexpected, unimaginably unfair loss. Either way, loving and losing has taken an incredible toll on you physically, mentally, and emotionally. Maybe you even resolved never to go through such turmoil again, steeling your heart against ever loving anyone enough to put you at risk of enduring that pain again.

That's a normal feeling. Catch your breath for a moment and let me tell you why you will—why you *must*—open your heart to love again.

- You owe it to yourself—and to others—to love. Romans 13:8 describes it as "the continuing debt to love one another" (NIV). That debt wasn't retired when your loved one died.

- Jesus is our example of loving even when that means pain and sacrifice: "Live a life filled with love, following the example of Christ. He loved us and offered himself as a sacrifice for us." When we follow His example, our lives can be "a pleasing aroma to God" (Ephesians 5:2).

- Loving others is the key to God's presence in our lives and His love being made complete in our lives: "Dear friends, since God so loved us, we also ought to love one another. . . . If we love one another, God lives in us and his love is made complete in us" (1 John 4:11–12 NIV).

- Love for others is the inescapable demonstration of God's presence in our lives: "The fruit of the Spirit is love" (Galatians 5:22 NIV).

- God doesn't want you to be afraid of the hurt that might come if you love again. Draw upon His love and strength, and you'll find more than enough to open your heart to love others. "God has not given us a spirit of fear and timidity, but of power, love, and self-discipline" (2 Timothy 1:7). And "there is no fear in love. But perfect love drives out fear" (1 John 4:18 NIV). This is what encouraged me to continue giving and receiving love, even after Ronald died. This verse loosed my chains of bondage and freed me to love again. It is my prayer that it does the same for you.

- You won't be betraying your departed loved one by loving again. You're not replacing him or her with someone else. Besides, remember how much that person loved you. He or she wouldn't want you to shut yourself off and be miserable and alone. Your loved one would want the best for you, want you to be happy and taken care of. Jesus, our example, made this clear. From the cross, He entrusted His beloved mother into the loving care of one of His closest friends, John, who took her into his home from that time on (see John 19:25–27).

- Even if you vowed never to love anyone else that much again, consider yourself off the hook. Your broken heart pulled back in fear and desperation. Your attempt to preserve yourself is understandable. Now, as time passes, know that loving others is the way to preserve and protect yourself. It's the way to move forward, the way to connect yourself to the human race, to life, and to God.

So go ahead and open yourself up to the possibility of love. No one can promise that you won't lose again, eventually, but imagine how many wonderful years of fellowship, support, camaraderie, and surprises you might cheat yourself out of if you isolate yourself. You might keep yourself from getting hurt again, but you'll also keep yourself from really living. You'll cheat yourself out of the future God wants to give you.

Rest assured, God knows how fragile your heart is right now. He knows what you need, and He knows how little you can bear. He's loving and gentle, no matter how bruised you feel, no matter how spent the smoldering embers of your heart: "A bruised reed he will not break, and a smoldering wick he will not snuff out" (Isaiah 42:3 NIV).

Have you ever wanted to close yourself off from those around you to avoid the pain of further loss? Why does it feel safer to remain detached?

_____

_____

_____

_____

_____

_____

Closing our hearts off from love locks us into ourselves and keeps us separated from other loved ones and from the world in which we live. Refusing to risk loving makes it impossible to receive what we need to survive during times of grief. When we enter into a winter season of our lives, our hope of survival sometimes depends on the love we give, the love we receive, and even the beautiful memories of loving and being loved.

Being open to love is the only way to truly live. We must let down our guard in order to initiate the healing process. Shutting down makes us unable even to fondly remember our loved one as we allow pain to swallow us whole.

I know that being this open makes us vulnerable, especially during the sensitive time of grief. But if you open your heart to this type of healing—to giving and receiving love—you will discover grace to deal with your grief.

How have you felt loved by those who stood by you during the grieving process? How did their outpouring of love make your pain more bearable?

_____

_____

_____

_____

_____

_____

_____

I want to challenge and encourage you to abandon any defenses you may have built that prevent you from giving and receiving love. Your choice to continue living your life with love will outlast your pain. A life of love will flood out the ache that is still in your heart. And it will leave you with joy.

Yes, loving hurts. Yet we choose to embrace love in spite of the inevitable pain of loss, because loving is living. The rewards of love are so worthwhile—so essential to life and happiness—that to fully have either, we must embrace loving others.

Whom have you been shutting out or holding at arm's length for fear that your heart might be broken if you open it? Is God calling you to embrace them and draw them into your heart?

How will you respond?

_____

_____

_____

_____

_____

_____

What's one thing you can do today to accept the risk of reaching out in love to someone God has sent into your life?

_____

_____

_____

_____

_____

_____

_____

_____

_____

_____

_____

_____

_____

_____

A Prayer for You

Dear Lord,

Hold our hands as we journey through the road of grief. Help us to follow the way of love as You demonstrated it through Your only Son, Jesus. Do not allow fear of pain to blind us or keep us from giving and receiving love. Take the lead in our lives and show us the right way. Enable us to trust in Your example and to live our lives in freedom, selflessly and openly. Teach us to love like You love, O Lord. Put us on a path that gives us a future of no regrets. Amen.

To love at all is to be vulnerable. Love anything, and your heart will certainly be wrung and possibly broken. If you want to make sure of keeping it intact, you must give your heart to no one, not even to an animal. Wrap it carefully round with hobbies and little luxuries; avoid all entanglements; lock it up safe in the casket or coffin of your selfishness. But in that casket—safe, dark, motionless, airless—it will change. It will not be broken; it will become unbreakable, impenetrable, irredeemable.

—C. S. LEWIS

Science has found that nothing can disappear without a trace. Nature does not know extinction. All it knows is transformation. If God applies the fundamental principle to the most minute and insignificant parts of the universe, doesn't it make sense to assume that He applies it to the masterpiece of His creation —the human soul? I think it does.

—WERNER VON BRAUN

CHAPTER SEVEN

The Eternal Spirit

Dear Ron,

After your death I realized that the spirit of a human being is more of a reality than even the temporal world. While the spirit is invisible to the naked eye, it is ever so present. It's like the wind. You can't see it, but you can feel it. Often you can even hear its gentle whispers or piercing cries. Perhaps this is why the Bible tells us to pay more attention to the things that are unseen. The apostle Paul reminded us to fix our eyes on what is unseen because what is seen is temporary, but the unseen is eternal.

Ronald, I'm sure you understand this reality, but this scripture has been quite an eye-opener for me. It made me aware that there is more to this life than what is visible to the naked eye. It made me realize that even though our human bodies are temporary, we are spirits, and as spirits we are eternal. This has encouraged me to live beyond the physical world in the sense of knowing that though you are not with me right now, we will see each other again.

Ronald, I know that your spirit is still very much alive. Maybe that's why it seems I can hear your thoughts about so many different things. Yes, I miss all of your physical attributes. I miss your face. I miss your hugs. I miss your smile. But I don't miss your spirit, because I can feel it through God's Spirit. And it is through God's Spirit that we are still and will be eternally connected.

Love, Angie

A Message for You

avid begged God to spare the child. He went without food and lay all
ght on the bare ground. The elders of his household pleaded with him
 get up and eat with them, but he refused. Then on the seventh day the
ild died. David's advisers were afraid to tell him. "He wouldn't listen to
ason while the child was ill," they said. "What drastic thing will he do
hen we tell him the child is dead?" When David saw them whispering,
 realized what had happened. "Is the child dead?" he asked. "Yes," they
plied, "he is dead." Then David got up from the ground, washed himself,
t on lotions, and changed his clothes. He went to the Tabernacle and
orshiped the LORD. After that, he returned to the palace and was served
od and ate. His advisers were amazed. "We don't understand you," they
d him. "While the child was still living, you wept and refused to eat. But
w that the child is dead, you have stopped your mourning and are eating
ain." David replied, "I fasted and wept while the child was alive, for I
id, 'Perhaps the LORD will be gracious to me and let the child live.' But
hy should I fast when he is dead? Can I bring him back again? I will go to
m one day, but he cannot return to me."

—2 Samuel 12:16–23

David's baby wasn't long for this world, but he's alive in heaven for all of eternity. What a marvelous hope and comfort it is for those of us who mourn the death of a loved one: death is not the end but only the beginning of the greatest part of our lives!

When one so young dies, mourning is different but no less painful than when losing a loved one in the prime of life. With babies or young children, we mourn the loss of promise and potential. We grieve not knowing what might have been; we grieve that we'll never really know them or see their personalities develop. Would he have been famous? Would she have been president or cured the common cold? Would she have looked like her mother, had her father's eyes, been tall like Grandpa? We feel cheated of the years we might have enjoyed together.

Whatever the age of the person we've lost, David's extraordinary example can inspire us both for his unwavering faith in God and for his crystal-clear understanding of life and death—and life again. For seven days, while his baby was ill, David fasted and prayed. He pleaded with God to spare the child. But when the boy died, rather than falling apart as people expected, given his intense reaction to the child's illness, David cleaned himself up so he could go to the tabernacle and worship the Lord. This was his first priority, even before eating after having fasted for seven days.

David's actions were difficult for his advisers to understand. But the great king understood the eternal nature of life and that his dead child lived on with God: "I will go to him one day," David spoke with faith and confidence. He grieved, but not "like people who have no hope" (1 Thessalonians 4:13). He would see his son again.

You may not be able to—or even want to—put your mourning in perspective so quickly or completely. That's okay. But isn't it a wonderful comfort to know that when we say "good-bye" to our loved ones who love the Lord, it's really only "see you later"? The body may die, but the spirit is eternal.

Isn't that knowledge comforting? While death separates us physically from those who have passed on, it does not take away the soul or the spirit of an individual. He or she has simply moved on to another place, to another space in time. Jesus Himself told those who didn't believe in life after death, "He is not the God of the dead, but of the living, for to him all are alive" (Luke 20:38 NIV).

We are more than bodies—more than blood, tissue, and muscle. We are more than our possessions. We are more than our accomplishments. We are spirits alive in Christ that even death cannot conquer. I once read a quote by Teilhard de Chardin: "We are not human beings having a spiritual experience. We are spiritual beings having a human experience."

How does it help you in your grief to remember that the proper focus is on the eternal, life in heaven, rather than on life here on earth?

_____

_____

_____

_____

_____

_____

Who's really more alive right now, you or the loved one who died and is with the Lord? How does that make you feel?

_____

_____

_____

_____

_____

_____

Being more spiritual than physical beings teaches me to focus more on eternal things than the things this world tries to fix my attention on—like keeping up with the Joneses, living in the right zip code, or looking like a supermodel. It reminds me to live my life with purpose and that life has more meaning than just how much stuff we have or what successes we may have achieved.

Not only that, but being committed to the spiritual, eternal

things of God is what gives us the strength and comfort to deal with the traumatic blows of life—even the agonizing pain of dealing with death. It helps us remember that, as Paul wrote, our troubles won't last long but will produce a glory that far outweighs the pain. "So we don't look at the troubles we can see now; rather, we fix our gaze on things that cannot be seen. For the things we see now will soon be gone, but the things we cannot see will last forever" (2 Corinthians 4:18).

Because we are spiritual beings in a spiritual life with Christ, we have hope in even the most tragic of circumstances. Yet because we are human, we still experience grief. Our hearts still ache with pain. This is why we must cling to God and devote our energies to seeking and trusting Him.

It helps when we recognize that our purpose is the same regardless of whether we are alive here on earth or in heaven: to honor the Lord. God's plan for you right now is to honor Him by remaining here, while God deemed it best for your loved one to honor Him in heaven. No matter how personal it feels when death comes calling, it's not all about us. As Paul said in Romans 14:7–9, "We don't live for ourselves or die for ourselves. If we live, it's to honor the Lord. And if we die, it's to honor the Lord. So whether we live or die, we belong to the Lord. Christ died and rose again for this very purpose—to be Lord both of the living and of the dead."

How do you believe God has been honored through your loved one's life and death? How has your response to the situation honored God? Is there something more God is calling you to do to honor Him with your life?

_____

_____

_____

_____

_____

_____

If only we could embrace eternity as we ought, our lives would be changed forever. We should be encouraged because the morning is coming when we can see things more clearly, a morning where fog and mist will be no more. The apostle Paul wrote, "Now we see things imperfectly as in a cloudy mirror, but then we will see everything with perfect clarity. All that I know now is partial and incomplete, but then I will know everything completely, just as God now knows me completely" (1 Corinthians 13:12). It won't be long before the weather clears and the sun shines bright, allowing us to see and understand it all. One day, we'll see as clearly as God does.

Knowing that our spirits never die helps me remember the precious bond I still share with my brother—the eternal, spiritual

bond that goes beyond physical presence into a dimension that I cannot fully comprehend. Jesus said that anyone who believes in Him will live, even after dying (see John 11:25). This is a divine privilege that all believers can look forward to. And this is what brings hope: a promise that someday we will again see those who have gone to be with the Lord before us.

How does knowing that we, as Christian believers, will live forever affect you? How does it affect the way you live? How does it affect you as it concerns the one you have lost?

_____

_____

_____

_____

_____

_____

_____

_____

_____

_____

_____

The writer of Ecclesiastes puts life here on earth into proper perspective: "The day you die is better than the day you are born" (Ecclesiastes 7:1); and, "Finishing is better than starting"

(Ecclesiastes 7:8). Of course, that's only true because of the hope we have in Christ, the promise of eternal life through Him.

The death of a loved one is never easy. We want them to be here with us. Death feels like an end—a terrible end that we didn't ask for and can barely endure. Yet it's not the end but rather a new beginning.

Because God is God of the living, and those who live for the Lord will never die, we can stay close to our loved ones forever. We can be assured that we haven't seen the last of our loved ones who are enjoying life in the presence of God. We can be confident that, although they cannot return to us, we can go to them. Someday we'll walk down streets of gold, where time has no end and neither do we, and be united once more with our beloved ones who have gone before us.

Reflections

A Prayer for You

Dear Lord,

Open our eyes to Your invisible world. Make it plain for us to see Your eternal Spirit. Guide our hearts through this temporal maze of life, and remind us of what is truly most important. Help us to value and cherish our relationships with others and our relationship with You. Lord, we are so grateful that You have come to give us everlasting life and that this gift can secure eternal relationships with those we love. Thank You for that gift of life that assures us that we have not been abandoned by others through death, but that through Your eternal life, we will one day see them again. Amen.

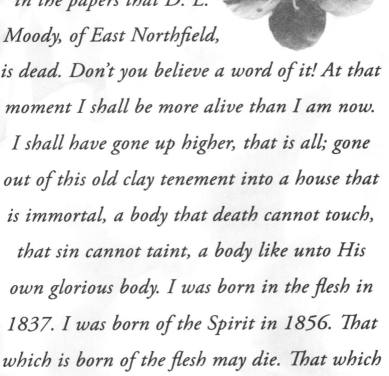

Someday you will read in the papers that D. L. Moody, of East Northfield, is dead. Don't you believe a word of it! At that moment I shall be more alive than I am now. I shall have gone up higher, that is all; gone out of this old clay tenement into a house that is immortal, a body that death cannot touch, that sin cannot taint, a body like unto His own glorious body. I was born in the flesh in 1837. I was born of the Spirit in 1856. That which is born of the flesh may die. That which is born of the Spirit will live forever.

—D. L. MOODY

Every Christian that goes before us from this world is a ransomed spirit waiting to welcome us in heaven.

—JONATHAN EDWARDS

CHAPTER EIGHT

When I See You Again

Dear Ron,

I can't recall ever writing you a letter, because there was never any distance between us that made it necessary. There was never a need to send updates about all the exciting things that happened in my life, because you were there with me during those times. I never had to describe some of the funniest TV commercials to you, because we witnessed them together. Not once did I tell you about the night I laughed my hardest, because you were the one that caused that laughter. And if by chance you weren't around, you were the first one I would call to share whatever I needed or wanted to share.

So, Ronald, can you imagine me trying to remember all the details of my life to share with you when I see you again? So much has happened. So much has changed. I could talk to you for days, and it still wouldn't be enough time. But don't worry, I'm holding on to all this information, because I know I will see you in heaven, and I know there will be a lot of catching up to do. I can't wait!

Ronald, I never imagined living my life without you, especially considering how much we've shared over the expanse of our lives. But I have such a blessed hope because of our promised heaven. I don't know what it will look like. I don't even know what you will look like. I just know you will be there. And we will be reunited. This is what makes me smile. You can't believe how I'm looking forward to that happy day!

Love, Angie

A Message for You

We know that when this earthly tent we live in is taken down (that is, when we die and leave this earthly body), we will have a house in heaven, an eternal body made for us by God himself and not by human hands. We grow weary in our present bodies, and we long to put on our heavenly bodies like new clothing. For we will put on heavenly bodies; we will not be spirits without bodies. While we live in these earthly bodies, we groan and sigh, but it's not that we want to die and get rid of these bodies that clothe us. Rather, we want to put on our new bodies so that these dying bodies will be swallowed up by life. God himself has prepared us for this, and as a guarantee he has given us his Holy Spirit. So we are always confident, even though we know that as long as we live in these bodies we are not at home with the Lord. For we live by believing and not by seeing. Yes, we are fully confident, and we would rather be away from these earthly bodies, for then we will be at home with the Lord.

—2 Corinthians 5:1–8

When you're grieving the death of one you love, "happily ever after" doesn't sound like it could possibly be the ending to your story. But for Christ's followers, it absolutely is! As 2 Corinthians 5:1 describes it, your loved one's "earthly tent" has been "taken down," but this is actually a positive development, not a heartless eviction. Believers in Jesus who die trade in their old tents for "a new house in heaven" made for them by God. Your loved one is moving up to a vastly better neighborhood with better accommodations and the very best neighbor of all, God Himself.

When someone we treasure dies, we are confronted by the fragility of the human body. It breaks down, wears out, ages, and weakens. We grapple with mortality—our own as well as our loved one's. Can you identify with how Paul describes life in these unreliable bodies in 2 Corinthians 5:2–4?

Paul said, "We grow weary in our present bodies, and we long to put on our heavenly bodies like new clothing" (verse 2). Have you ever felt weary in your body, particularly in the midst of the ordeal of losing and grieving? What excites you about the prospect of you and your loved one putting on new heavenly bodies like new and improved clothing?

_____

_____

_____

———————————————————————————————

———————————————————————————————

———————————————————————————————

———————————————————————————————

———————————————————————————————

Paul continued: "While we live in these earthly bodies, we groan and sigh, but it's not that we want to die and get rid of these bodies that clothe us. Rather, we want to put on our new bodies so that these dying bodies will be swallowed up by life" (verse 4).

Did you catch that? Your loved one's dying body has been swallowed up by life. As Paul explains it in 1 Corinthians 15:42–43, "Our earthly bodies are planted in the ground when we die, but they will be raised to live forever. Our bodies are buried in brokenness, but they will be raised in glory. They are buried in weakness, but they will be raised in strength."

If that sounds like it won't really be the same person you loved, be assured that it will be. And don't worry that you won't be able to recognize him or her. When Jesus, Moses, and Elijah spoke on the mountaintop in their transfigured, heavenly bodies (see Matthew 17:1–5), Jesus' disciples had no trouble recognizing all three—even though Moses and Elijah had lived centuries earlier, and in a time before photographs! It seems likely that who we really are on the inside, our spirits, will so shine through our new heavenly bodies that we'll be instantly recognizable as ourselves.

No matter how new and improved your loved one is in heaven, it'll still be that wonderful person you know and love—only better than he or she has ever been before.

Those who die with faith in the Lord make a remarkable trade: glory for their brokenness, strength for their weakness, life instead of death. Who can be sad for someone who has the good fortune of swinging that deal?

Paul understood what made life in heaven most attractive. In 2 Corinthians 5:8 Paul told the believers, "We would rather be away from these earthly bodies, for then we will be at home with the Lord." Rather? Is Paul actually saying that death is preferable to life on earth for believers? That's exactly what he's saying. We can't totally understand the magnitude of that attraction now, because we haven't yet experienced it; but the greatest joy of heaven will be the privilege of being at home—comfortable and safe—with the great God of the universe. One day we will be at our resting home, our true home, and it'll be God's house.

Jesus encouraged His loved ones to take comfort and courage from that fact when they were afraid or distressed: "Don't let your hearts be troubled. Trust in God, and trust also in me. There is more than enough room in my Father's home. If this were not so, would I have told you that I am going to prepare a place for you? When everything is ready, I will come and get you so that you will always be with me where I am" (John 14:1–3).

Your loved one's place is ready. And when your life is over, God will have a place prepared for you as well.

As we can see, the reality of heaven—new, strong bodies; being at home with the Lord—means that we need not grieve for our loved ones who have died. They've finished the hard part; their celebration has already started. The groaning and sighing they endured as part of the dying—or transformation—process has already been swallowed up in victory and in life. Who, then, is our grief really for? How can understanding what the Bible teaches about our life after death comfort those grieving a loved one's death? What most comforts you?

_____

_____

_____

_____

_____

_____

_____

_____

The death of believers is bittersweet. We grieve the loss of them on earth, while they're walking down streets of gold without pain, without doubt, without sadness. On the one hand, the emptiness of life without them hurts; on the other hand, they are alive and well in eternal paradise. It's both heartbreaking and comforting.

How has the reality of heaven encouraged you after your loved one's death? In what specific ways is his or her death bittersweet?

_____

_____

_____

_____

_____

_____

Heaven is the final destination for all who believe in Jesus. Isn't this something worth looking forward to? We'll be with Jesus, and we'll be reunited with our loved ones forever after we die. We will see again those we have lost. We'll get to hug them and hold their hands and tell them how much we love and have missed them. I don't know about you, but that tickles me. Knowing I will see Ronald again gives me a strength deep within to keep on living my life as best I can.

Heaven will be the venue for the greatest reunion in history. Not only will we see our loved ones again, but we will get to meet the saints of old—biblical figures like Job, Moses, Joshua, David, Lazarus, Mary, Peter, Dorcas, and Paul. It will be quite the celebration.

Close your eyes and imagine heaven. What do you think it will look like? Whom do you envision meeting again? Take a few moments to picture this paradise, and then describe that image in the space below.

_____

_____

_____

_____

_____

_____

Before your loved one died, you might not have given heaven much thought. But now it's likely you think about it a lot. Although we might wish we could know more than the Bible tells us (we'd like a video clip with all the sights and sounds of heaven), there's quite a lot we actually can know. Because what we're told of heaven and life after death is taught in small pieces in various books of the Bible, it can be a little confusing. Basically, the timeline goes something like this:

- When a Christian dies, he steps instantly into the presence of Jesus, while his body is buried in the ground. He enters eternal life in a glorified, transfigured body similar to the body Jesus had after He rose from the dead but before He returned to heaven (see John 20:19–20).

- At the second coming of Jesus, our returning Lord will "bring back with him the believers who have died" (1 Thessalonians 4:14). At the Lord's commanding shout, with the voice of the archangel, and with the trumpet call of God, the bodies of Christians who have died will be resurrected immortal, incorruptible, and perfect. Christians who are alive will be caught up into the clouds to join with them and meet the Lord in the air (see 1 Thessalonians 4:13–18).

- You and I—and your loved ones and mine—will enjoy life together forever in heaven with God.

And what will heaven be like? In Revelation God gives us just enough insight to whet our appetites for the joys of heaven:

- Heaven is a place where nothing will be lost, damaged, or ruined. "Store your treasures in heaven, where moths and rust cannot destroy, and thieves do not break in and steal" (Matthew 6:20).

- Never again will you lose someone you love. Never again will you grieve or feel sorrow or pain. That's because heaven is a place without tears, without pain, without heartbreak, without sadness. God "will wipe every tear from their eyes, and there will be no more death or sorrow or crying or pain. All these things are gone forever" (Revelation 21:4).

- Heaven is a place of ultimate renewal for both spirit and body. What was broken will be made whole. What was old and worn out will be made fresh and new. "The one sitting

on the throne said, 'Look, I am making everything new!'"
(Revelation 21:5).

- Heaven is a place where there will be no evil, jealousy,
lying, stealing, bullying, or immorality. "Nothing evil will
be allowed to enter, nor anyone who practices shameful
idolatry and dishonesty" (Revelation 21:27).

Heaven will be a place of ultimate restoration in every way
possible, even in ways we can't yet imagine. It is a paradise of
vast proportions where joy and peace reside and where God
sits on His throne. The book of Revelation (chapter 21) goes
into extraordinary specifics about the beauty and splendor of
heaven—streets of gold, city gates hewn from gigantic solid
pearls, its source of light being the glory of God, and walls
adorned with precious stones. Heaven is a place of unparalleled
beauty.

Read the description of heaven in Revelation 21 and 22.
What most stands out to you, delights you, encourages you?

_____

_____

_____

_____

_____

_____

_____

What do you think will be most appealing to your loved one who is already present with the Lord in heaven?

_____

_____

_____

_____

_____

_____

Write a message to God about heaven. Tell Him what you're looking forward to and what thoughts you wish you could pass on to your loved one who is with Him. Don't be afraid to be honest about your fears about death, your questions about heaven, and the difficulty you're experiencing after the death of one you loved so much. Ask Him to help you through this time, comfort you, and make the truth of heaven extraordinarily real to you.

_____

_____

_____

_____

_____

_____

_____

Reflections

A Prayer for You

Dear Lord,

How encouraging it is to know that our loved ones are in Your care. Knowing they are safe in Your arms gives us great peace of mind and fills us with joy divine. Thank You for the blessed hope of eternal paradise, where we will not only see those who have gone before us, but we will experience life ever after in Your holy and sweet presence. Help us to live our lives in anticipation of this great gift. Help us to finish the great race of life as champions, as You have intended us to do. Give us strength and whatever we need to triumphantly endure to the end. Amen.

What delight will it afford to renew the sweet counsel we have taken together, to recount the toils of combat and the labour of the way, and to approach, not the house, but the throne of God in company, in order to join in the symphonies of heavenly voices, and lose ourselves amid the splendours and fruitions of the beatific vision!

—ROBERT HALL